To

Eden

From

mrsam

Date

Standard
BIBLE STORYBOOK SERIES

JESUS
THE EARLY YEARS

Retold by Carolyn Larsen

Standard®
PUBLISHING

Cincinnati, Ohio

Published by Standard Publishing, Cincinnati, Ohio
www.standardpub.com
Copyright © 2012 by Standard Publishing

Printed in: China

Project editors: Elaina Meyers, Dawn A. Medill, and Marcy Levering
Cover design: Dale Meyers

Illustrations from Standard Publishing's Classic Bible Art Collection

ISBN 978-0-7847-3525-1

Library of Congress Cataloging-in-Publication Data

Larsen, Carolyn, 1950-
  Jesus : the early years / retold by Carolyn Larsen.
      p. cm.
  ISBN 978-0-7847-3525-1
1. Jesus Christ--Biography--Juvenile literature. 2. Bible stories,
English--N.T. Gospels. I. Title.
  BT302.L286 2012
  232.9'01--dc23
  [B]
                          2011051537

17 16 15 14 13 12   1 2 3 4 5 6 7 8 9

Jesus Is Born

God gave John the Baptist the job of announcing that Jesus was coming to do God's work on earth. His plan was to send Jesus to earth as a human being. Jesus entered the world just as everyone does—as an infant. Jesus' birth had miracles all around it because, after all, He was leaving the royalty of Heaven behind. He didn't come to earth in a palace just so rich people could know Him. His birth was simple, just as the prophets had predicted.

An Angel Speaks to Mary *Luke 1:26-38*

Elizabeth was six months pregnant when the same angel who had promised her a baby made a visit to a young woman named Mary. This young woman was engaged to be married to a man named Joseph. He was a carpenter, and way back in his family tree was the great King David. Gabriel appeared to Mary and said, "Mary, God is very happy with you!"

Mary was confused by this statement. She couldn't figure out what the angel meant so she was afraid. "Don't be frightened," the angel said. "God has decided to bless you in a wonderful way! He has decided that you will have a baby . . . a son whom you will name Jesus. This baby will be very great and will be the Son of God himself. God will give this child the throne of King David. He will reign over Israel forever! His kingdom will never end!"

Mary was amazed but also confused. "How can I have a baby?" she asked. "I'm not even married."

The angel told her that God's power would make her pregnant. "The baby you have will be the Son of God," said Gabriel. Then the angel told her that her cousin, Elizabeth, was also going to have a baby. "People used to say that she would never have a baby because she's already so old, but nothing is impossible with God."

Mary thought about everything the angel said. She thought about how much she loved God. Then she said, "I will do whatever the Lord wants. I am His servant." When the angel heard this he left her.

Jesus Is Born *Matthew 1:18-25; Luke 2:1-7*

Right after the angel Gabriel came to tell Mary that she was going to have a baby, God's angel also visited Joseph. "Joseph, the girl you are engaged to marry is going to have a baby. But the baby she is having is God's Son. Don't be afraid to go ahead and marry her. She is a woman who has found great favor with God. When the baby is born, name Him Jesus because He will save His people from their sins."

When Joseph woke up he did exactly what the angel said; he married Mary.

A short time later, the Roman emperor decided he wanted to know how many people lived in his kingdom. To find out that number, he ordered that a count of all the people in the land be taken. People had to go back to the towns their ancestors had once lived in to be counted. That meant that Joseph had to go to the city of Bethlehem where his ancestor

8

King David had lived. Joseph left Nazareth with Mary. It was a difficult trip for Mary because she was ready to have a baby any day.

When they arrived in Bethlehem, the little town was crowded with people who had come to be counted. Joseph had trouble finding a place for them to stay. They ended up staying in a stable because there was no room in the inn. That very night Mary gave birth to her baby. She and Joseph named Him Jesus, just as the angel had told them to do. When the little boy was born, Mary wrapped Him tightly in strips of cloth and laid Him in the animal's feedbox.

Shepherds Visit Jesus *Luke 2:8-20*

The same night that Mary gave birth to Jesus some shepherds in a field outside of Bethlehem had an interesting experience. Late that night, the shepherds were watching for animals that might hurt their sleeping sheep. The night was dark and quiet but suddenly the sky above them lit up with the presence of God's angel! The glory of God filled the whole sky so that it was as light as daytime. The shepherds were amazed when the angel spoke to them. "Do not be afraid," the angel said. "I have

wonderful news for you! God's Son has been born tonight in the village of Bethlehem. He is your Savior, Christ the Lord. You will find Him wrapped in strips of cloth and lying in an animal's feedbox."

The shepherds were even more amazed when a whole host of angels filled the sky. They all praised God saying, "Glory to God in the highest, and peace on earth to all men on whom God's favor rests!"

When the angels left, the shepherds were filled with excitement. "Let's go to Bethlehem and find the baby they were talking about!" they said. So they hurried to Bethlehem and found the baby who was lying in the feedbox just as the angel said. The shepherds were amazed by this and they told everyone they met about the baby and what the angel told them about Him. Mary listened to everything they said about Jesus and she kept all these things in her heart and mind. As the shepherds returned to their work in the fields, they praised God and glorified Him for this wonderful gift.

Wise Men Visit Jesus *Matthew 2:1-12*

Sometime after Jesus was born a special star appeared in the sky over a country to the east of Judah. Some wise men saw the star and they knew that it meant a new king had been born. So the wise men packed gifts to give the king and began traveling.

The star moved slowly through the sky and the wise men followed it. The star led them to Jerusalem where the wise men went to visit King Herod. "Where is the new king of the Jews?" they asked. "We saw His star in the sky and have followed it here."

King Herod was very angry to hear that there was a new king. He asked the wise men many questions about the star and what it meant. The wise men told him what the prophets had taught about a new king of the Jews. So he told the wise men to go on to Bethlehem and look for the king there. "Please return to me and tell me where this king is so that I can go worship Him too," King Herod asked.

The star began moving again so the wise men followed it all the way to Bethlehem. The star stopped right over the house where Jesus lived with Joseph and Mary. The wise men bowed to the young king and gave Him the gifts they had brought for Him: gold, sweet smelling frankincense, and a perfume called myrrh. When the wise men left Bethlehem they did not go back to Jerusalem to report to King Herod. God warned them in a dream to stay away from the king because he wanted to hurt the child, not worship Him.

Escape to Egypt *Matthew 2:13-23*

ot long after the wise men left, God appeared to Joseph in a dream. "Get up right now," God said, "take Mary and Jesus and get out of Judah. Run to Egypt because King Herod wants to hurt Jesus. In fact, he is going to search for the child and try to kill Him. Stay in Egypt until I tell you it is safe to come back."

Joseph went right away and got Mary and Jesus up, even though it was the middle of the night, and they escaped to Egypt. They stayed there until God came to Joseph in another dream and told him it was safe to return to Judah.

When King Herod realized that the wise men had tricked him by going home another way he was very angry! He wanted to make sure that this new king of the Jews didn't take his kingdom so he ordered that all the little boys in or near Bethlehem who were two years old or younger be killed! That would cover all the boy babies from the time the wise men had come to see him until the present. It was a terrible time. Mothers begged for their sons to be saved and sobbed and cried when they weren't.

When King Herod died, the angel of God told Joseph it was safe to take Jesus home because those who were trying to hurt Him were dead. Joseph took Mary and Jesus to Nazareth, because he heard that another bad king was ruling in the area where they had lived before. This made the prophecy true that Jesus would be called a Nazarene—one who was from Nazareth.

JESUS GROWING UP

Jesus grew up in the little village of Nazareth. Joseph was a carpenter so Jesus may have learned carpentry from him. The Bible does not give much information about Jesus' childhood. But the story of when He went to Jerusalem with His mother and father to attend the Passover Feast celebration is an important one. That trip reminded Mary and Joseph that there was something special about their son.

The Boy in the Temple *Luke 2:41-52*

Every year Jesus' parents traveled to Jerusalem for the Passover Feast celebration. The year that Jesus was 12 years old they made the trip as usual and when the feast was over the family left for home. Mary and Joseph were walking with a large group of family and friends. They assumed Jesus was somewhere in the group. They didn't

know that He had actually stayed behind in Jerusalem. After the group had been walking for a while, Mary and Joseph looked for Jesus but they couldn't find Him anywhere. They quickly turned around and went right back to Jerusalem. The worried couple looked everywhere for the young boy. They searched everywhere they had been. They searched places He might have been curious about. They looked and looked for three days but didn't find Him anywhere. Finally on the third day they found Jesus. He was in the temple with the wise and educated teachers. He was listening to them talk and asking them questions. Everyone in the temple was amazed at how

wise He was and what good questions He asked. Jesus not only asked good questions, He had good answers for their questions.

Mary went right up to Jesus and asked Him, "Why did You do this? Your father and I have been very worried about You. We've been searching everywhere in the city for You!"

"Why were you searching everywhere for me?" Jesus answered.

"You should have known that I would be in my Father's house." Mary and Joseph didn't understand what He meant. But Jesus went home to Nazareth with them. He obeyed them and honored them as His parents. Mary thought about this incident often as she watched Jesus grow into a young man. Everyone liked Him and He honored and obeyed God in all He did.

THE MINISTRY OF JOHN

It was a miracle that John was born to his elderly parents. But God had special work for the son of Zechariah to do. John paved the way . . . he let people know that Jesus, God's Son, was coming. John told the people to get ready to hear Jesus' message and to learn from Him!

A Strange Man *Matthew 3:1-12; Luke 3:1-16*

G od gave John the Baptist a special job to do. He traveled around in the wilderness outside of towns and preached about Jesus! He told the people, "Turn away from your sins and turn to God because the kingdom of Heaven is near." The Old Testament prophet Isaiah wrote that a messenger would come ahead of God's Son and would let people know that God's Son was coming. John was that messenger.

John was an unusual man. He wore clothes made from camel's hair with a leather belt around his waist. He ate locusts and wild honey. But even though he was odd, people came from all over to hear John preach. People listened to him and confessed their sins and repented of them, then John baptized them in the Jordan River. That's how he got the name John the Baptist.

One time John saw some of the leaders of the temple coming to be baptized and he knew what their hearts were like. "You are a bunch of snakes!" he said. "Show by the way you live that you have truly repented of your sins. Don't assume that you are automatically safe from God's judgment just because your ancestor was Abraham. Don't you see that

God is ready to chop you off from His family? He cuts down every tree that doesn't produce fruit."

John continued with, "I baptize you with water, when you turn away from your sins, but there is One coming after me who is far greater and more powerful and important than I am. I am not even worthy to be His servant but He will baptize you with the Holy Spirit. He will separate the useful people from those who aren't serious about knowing and serving God."

"What do we do?" the people asked. "How do we show God we're serious about this?"

"If you have two coats, give one to someone who has none," John said. "If you have food, share it with someone who has none."

Dishonest tax collectors came too, to have John baptize them. "Stop being dishonest," John told them. "Treat people fairly." Many people listened to John and turned away from their sins and followed God.

Jesus Is Baptized

Matthew 3:13-17; Mark 1:9-11;
Luke 3:21, 22; John 1:29-34

One day John was preaching to people near the town of Bethany and baptizing many of them in the Jordan River. While he was baptizing, Jesus came up to him. "I want you to baptize me," He said. "I can't baptize You," John said. "I am the one who should be baptized by You. Why are You asking me to do this?"

Jesus answered gently, "I must do everything in the right way. Please baptize me." So John led Jesus out into the waters of the Jordan River and he baptized Him. As John lifted Jesus up out of the water, the clouds above them divided and a dove flew down and settled on Jesus. It was God's Holy Spirit! Then a voice spoke from Heaven. God said, "This is my

Son. I love Him very much and I'm very happy with Him!" The next day John saw Jesus again. He pointed toward Jesus and announced to all the people near by, "Look, there is the Lamb of God who will take away all our sins! He is the One I've been talking about when I said that some- one was coming who is greater than I am. I didn't know that He was the One until I baptized Him. Then I saw the Holy Spirit come and rest on Him and a voice from Heaven said that He is God's Son! I saw this happen. I know for certain that He is the One I've been preaching about!"

Preparation for Ministry

John the Baptist baptized Jesus and now Jesus was ready to begin His work for God. He was about 30 years old and God had some important work for Him to do. It wasn't always going to be easy . . . in fact, the first thing that happened showed how difficult His work was going to be!

Jesus Is Tempted

Matthew 4:1-11; Mark 1:12, 13; Luke 4:1-13

After Jesus was baptized He left the area around the Jordan River. It was time for His work for God to begin but something else had to happen first. The Spirit of God led Him out into the wilderness where the devil met Him. They were there in the wilderness together for 40 days and 40 nights. That whole time the devil was tempting Jesus to turn away from God. Jesus ate no food for that whole 40 days which, of course, meant that He was very hungry.

"If You are really the Son of God,"

the devil said, "then take these stones here on the ground and change them into bread."

"No!" Jesus said. "The Scriptures tell us that people need more than just bread to have a good life."

The devil had another plan. He took Jesus to the temple in Jerusalem.

They went to the highest part of the building and the devil said, "If You are really God's Son, then jump off. I know that the Scriptures say that God orders His angels to take care of You; so they will catch You and even keep You from hurting yourself at all."

"Yes, well the Scriptures also say that You shouldn't test the Lord your God!" Jesus said. The devil knew then that he wasn't going to make any progress with this temptation, but he wasn't finished with Jesus.

Then the devil took Jesus to a very high place. He showed Him all the nations of the world; all the land and all the people. "I will give You all of this to rule," the devil said. "You will have glory and power and authority over these kingdoms. I can do this because I have authority over all of them. I can give them to anyone I please. I will give it all to You if You will just bow down and worship me," the devil said.

"I will not because I know that the Scriptures say to worship God and God alone and to only serve Him. I will not bow down to you," Jesus answered.

Jesus Calls His Disciples

Matthew 4:18-22; 9:9-13; Mark 1:14-20; 2:14-17; Luke 5:1-11; 27-32; John 1:35-51

J esus began His ministry for God by teaching people about His Father. He challenged people to turn away from their sins and obey God. Many people followed Jesus—either because they believed Him and what He taught or because they were curious about Him. Jesus chose 12 men to be His special students. They are called Jesus'

disciples. Most of the men He called to follow Him were fishermen. Some He saw working on their nets and He called them to follow Him. One time He was teaching some people as He stood on the shore of a lake. The crowd of people pressed in on Him so He was nearly pushed into the water. Jesus saw a couple of fishing boats nearby so He climbed into one of them and taught the crowd from there. The fishermen were a little ways off washing their nets after working all night. When Jesus was finished teaching the people, He told the fisherman (who owned the boat He was sitting in) to push the boat out into deeper water and fish some more.

"Sir, we worked hard the whole night," the fisherman named Simon said, "and we didn't catch even one fish. But because You say so, I'll go fishing again." The fisherman pushed the boat out into the water and dropped his nets. Immediately the nets were filled with so many fish that Simon had to call for help in order to pull the nets up. Simon was amazed. He realized that Jesus was no ordinary man. "I'm too much of a sinner to be around You. Please leave me!" Simon begged.

"Don't be afraid," Jesus said. "Follow me and I'll show you how to fish for people!" Simon left his boat right there and followed Jesus.

Another time, Jesus saw a tax collector sitting in his booth collecting tax money from the people. Most people hated tax collectors because many of them were dishonest and collected extra money to keep for themselves. But Jesus turned to this tax collector, named Matthew, and said, "Come and follow me!" Matthew got up right away and followed Jesus. Later Matthew hosted a big banquet for many of his tax collector friends and Jesus attended it too. The religious leaders criticized Jesus for being with the hated tax collectors. But Jesus said, "Healthy people are not the ones who need a doctor; sick people need doctors. I have come to challenge sinners to stop sinning and that is why I spend time with sinners. I don't want to spend time with people who believe they are already good enough for God."

Jesus finished calling His 12 special disciples. Their names were Peter, Andrew (Peter's brother), James, John, Philip, Bartholomew, Matthew, Thomas, James, Simon, Judas, and Judas Iscariot.

JESUS' MINISTRY BEGINS

The preparation was done. Jesus experienced what it felt like to be truly tempted to turn away from God. He began teaching about obeying God and had many people following Him. He also had chosen His 12 special students who would be with Him every step of the way. Now it was time to take His ministry and work to the next level. Big things were about to happen!

A Wedding in Cana *John 2:1-11*

Mary, Jesus' mother, was invited to a wedding celebration in the town of Cana. Jesus and His disciples were invited to the wedding too. Wedding celebrations went on for days and days. It was a big party for many people! Part way through this celebration though, there was a problem. The host of the party ran out of wine. Wine was the main beverage for the party and it would be a disgrace for the host to run out before the party was over. Mary heard that the host had this problem and she wanted to help him. The only thing Mary could think of was to go to her son. So she pulled Jesus aside and told Him, "They have no more wine."

"That's too bad," Jesus said. "But I can't do anything about it. The time for me to do miracles hasn't come yet."

But Mary just ignored what He said. She turned to some servants standing nearby and instructed them to do whatever Jesus told them to do.

There were six large stone pitchers nearby. They were big pitchers that each held 20 or 30 gallons of water but they were empty at the moment. Jesus pointed to the pitchers and told the servants to fill them up with water. When the pitchers were all filled, Jesus told a servant to dip out some of the water and take it to the host of the celebration.

When the man tasted what the servant brought him, he was amazed! It was no longer water. It was the most delicious and most expensive wine he had ever tasted. He didn't know where it had come from (although the servant knew). The host called the bridegroom over and said, "Usually people serve the best wine first and then cheaper wine later. But you have definitely saved the best for last!"

Of course the bridegroom had no idea what the man was talking about.

He didn't know that Jesus had just performed the first miracle of His ministry on earth by changing the water into wine. When the disciples saw what Jesus did, they believed that He was a special man and that the power of God was with Him!

Jesus Clears the Temple *John 2:13-25*

It was time for the annual Passover Celebration so Jesus went to Jerusalem. It was the custom for people to come to the temple and offer sacrifices to God. But when Jesus came into the temple courts, He saw merchants selling cattle, sheep, and doves. The people were buying the animals so they had sacrifices to offer. But the merchants were charging very high prices to the poor people. Jesus was angry that these merchants were making a profit from the poor people who just wanted to honor God.

Jesus grabbed some ropes and made a whip out of them. He snapped the whip and chased the merchants out of the temple and scattered the animals. Then He turned over the tables of the moneychangers who were cheating the people too. He shouted, "Get out of here! Do not turn my Father's house into a marketplace!"

The temple leaders got very angry at Him. "What right do You have to come in here and do these things? If You truly have the authority from God to do this, then show us some miraculous sign!"

Jesus answered, "Destroy this temple and I will raise it back up again in three days!"

"What are You talking about?" the Jewish leaders asked. "It took 46 years to build this temple and You think You can do it in three days?" They didn't understand that Jesus was not talking about the temple building. He was talking about His own body. He was saying that His body would be raised back to life three days after He died. His disciples remembered this after He was actually raised from the dead and they believed in Him and in the Scriptures.

Because of the miracles Jesus did in Jerusalem during the Passover, many people believed that He was the Messiah.

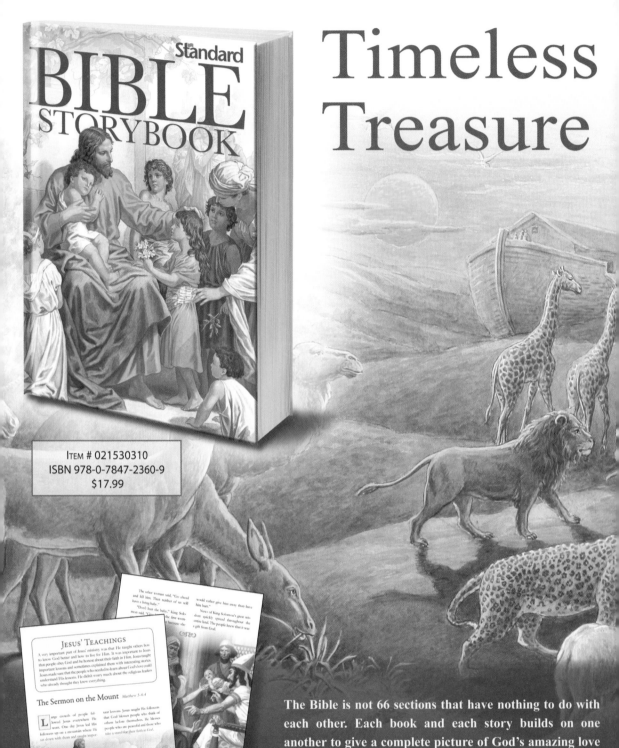